Thorn

By the same author:

Poetry
Woodsmoke

Thorn

Todd Turner

PUNCHER & WATTMANN

First published in 2020
Published by Puncher and Wattmann
PO Box 279
Waratah NSW 2298

http://www.puncherandwattmann.com
puncherandwattmann@bigpond.com

NATIONAL
LIBRARY
OF AUSTRALIA

A catalogue record for this book is available from the National Library of Australia

ISBN   978195780635

Cover image: Guy Maestri   Wreck No. 4   2015   oil on linen   51.0 x 61.0 cm
Image courtesy of Jan Murphy Gallery.
Cover design: David Musgrave

Printed by Lightning Source International

Contents

for Alanah

The trick is in the making
not the made
—John Burnside

The craft of singing
recruits apprentices from the abyss
—Michael Dransfield

What sap
went through that little thread
to make the cherry red!
—Marianne Moore

1

Thread

A pulse, an inkling. Numinous wellings.
Filament that seems to emerge inborn.
And like the mind waking in the skin
of its own thoughts, all illumined and still,
you follow that lit trail and allow yourself
to leave the spool of your body clock

ticking behind. And in the space that fills
with more air than light you traipse
what appears to be the backwoods
of an unremembered wilderness,
journeying more out of hope than quest
for mere trace, prints in long gone ground.

Though it takes something more or less
like groundwork for the tracks to reappear
in the vein and slipstream of a path
made unfamiliar to you now. Still,
you forage the pith and purblind chamber,
the heart hauled bloodlines of inherent bone.

And out of the marrowing absence comes
an undertow, tinctured within the weight,
a kind of nothingness that's been threading
away in the silt and sinew of some buried truth,
like the pause before the breathless becoming
of a word that draws on its implicit shape.

My Middle Name

1

The sound of my middle name is silence—
my birthright by my mother's reckoning.

We were bound by the broken bond,
the standoff between my mother

and her father. As far back as I can remember,
words about my grandfather surfaced in whispers

and when they broke from my mother's lips,
I listened to the breaking solitude of those storms.

Driven by rain and tempered by drought,
I pictured an emptiness she longed to fill

with the fixed aim of her tender intent.
Since the moment she fled, she stared down

those days, focused, unforgiven—determined
to break from the iron glare of her father's will.

2

I like to imagine my mother and father
making their way for Bathurst Station.

I like to think how they borrowed his
father's Buick, how they called,

once they made the station, to let him know
of its whereabouts and where they were headed.

I like to think of them together on the platform,
alone and on the run, hungry with hope and need.

This was the night they fled. This was the moment
they planned on leaving the wreckage behind.

Many times I've imagined them watching
the lights of the train come grinding to a halt.

The doors open, they step into the carriage,
the train slips into the fog and they are gone.

3

Before long, my mother's father
trailed the shining steel his daughter took

as a life line out. He must have cursed
her all the way down the barrel of those tracks.

Pissed off and on edge, he would have ridden
the bullet of his own breath, swallowed

his stricken pride with restrained fury.
The further the train pulled away from the Plains'

red-dark horizon, the more his bitterness
would have sharpened in his mouth.

I can taste it now, as I picture my grandfather
stepping off the train, country-link side,

Central Station, the ghost of his unspeakable grief
ploughing the newfound fertility of his burden.

4

My grandfather never spoke of his father's death.
Suicide is a dead farm, a nameless grave.

Still, it must have emanated in every gesture
of his being. In letters between my mother

and her sisters, a three word phrase confides
—*Don't tell father.* Home on the farm,

silence was a whip, a tight-lipped line.
A taut knot, it could tie anything off:

boundaries, fences, bullocks, deadwood.
Out there, what lingered unspoken was Word.

My grandfather silenced his father away.
My mother wanted to rid herself of his habit of pain.

They were hollowed by the sound that caged
them in distance and I was born in its name.

5

When my mother next saw her father
it was from the back of a tram.

Chance rallied like fate coming into being.
My father, the tram conductor, was issuing tickets.

My grandfather had never set foot in a city.
Trams were a cattle run for standing stock.

My father lowered his hat as my grandfather
clambered on board. Oblivious,

he took the ticket and moved along.
My mother hid behind a passenger

carrying her first unborn, while my father
turned his back and hunched beneath

his tie and coat. My grandfather was holding
a summons, stamped with a date for court.

6

The double doors to the courthouse
were halved as they entered it,

gloss over wood knots and the grain.
The air was shackled with a code

my mother knew from her girlhood home.
My father was set to speak the truth.

To the judge, measure was the unwritten
letter of the law and he could gauge

from the shouts of debt and betrayal,
that my mother's father bore an old-growth

bloodline, the cost and curfew of affliction.
When the judge delivered his ruling,

he grafted his measure and splayed a lineage
as if to raise a leaf from tangled shoots.

7

Many times I found my mother trying
to air the echo of her father's silence.

Often alone at the sink in the kitchen,
her gloved hands soaked, finning the boil.

But it was in the garden, kneeling
over weeds and perennials, and always

while digging or plying an axe,
where she'd spell out the sum of her piece.

I listened for a link between the terms
which couldn't be buried or bridged

and what I heard was the unbending
halves of two truths. Two truths.

One separateness. A father and daughter.
Together apart, in the gulf of their undoing.

8

When frustrations pulsed high and talk became low,
when the past would warp and weigh-in heavily,

I'd sit with my mother in swallowed silence.
In her breath, I could hear her recalibrate her senses

through the blunt and level stations of her stare.
She'd churn all she was ever denied

by her father to settle her own truth over time.
My middle name was born from absence,

from generations of longing and distance.
All that had been torn apart by loss

could never be salvaged or squared by a name.
My mother swore not to place a value on what was lost.

She only longed for what she could change
in the ache of making good from what she was given.

Tiny Ruins

Out of season and running against the grain,
the wind pummels the windows with such force
that the glass shudders like a rack of wobble
boards. I press my ear to the gyprock

and listen to the updraft bellow
in the stairwell shaft. I peel back the blinds
and see trees buckled over like journeymen
up against it on the ropes. Someone should

throw in the towel. A bulb blows, a screw
pops and a picture frame falls from the wall.
I tiptoe around the tiny ruins and step outside.
Dark air invisibly ropes me with hefty knots.

I offer no guard—and watch a bin topple and slide
down the lane, as another, cartwheeling end over
end, tosses its trash like confetti, while a fledgling
fence-bird sharpens its beak, scratching in disregard.

The Raft

Wild with whatever the suburban blue
dished-up for a summer's day,
we took the dog and dragged the inflatable raft
from its corner of neglect in the shed.
We wrestled it free from a hoard of rakes
which had it pinned, half-slumped, to the wall,
then lurched it out into the open, our
restless skins churning in the hull of our bones.
The raft was a sarcophagus at first, tinselled
with dead bugs and leaves. Out on the lawn
it was a slovenly drunk who needed to be shaken
into shape and sobriety. We hosed it off
then jamming the valve in its mouth while pumping,
it sat up, took a deep breath, coughed up a nasty
dribble of spit, and finally started to breathe.
We lugged it over the fence and shouldered
it down the road. To passers-by, we must
have looked like ferals set to a ragtime tune,
or playacting pallbearers in a funeral parade.
But we were hitchers, strays, stragglers smudging
our prints into the cracks of trodden gloom.
We edged our way, barefoot, beyond the glare
of deadend streets, on paths of burning tar,
heading towards the place where the burb-belt
broke away from its fripperies, where the sound
of creekwater lured us like fish into one of its pools.
At the brink, all four of us gripped the raft
and wearing it like a hat, waddled beneath
a jungled weft of elephantine branches
then descending the embankment, we stood

in the thick of it and couldn't make head
or tail of where we were. We started to believe
the raft would snag and blow. It didn't—
and once clear, we dropped it into the deep end.
There, we were out of bounds and far from reach,
free from gravity's grip. In the creek, the raft
was a thing unto itself, swilling in concentric rings.
I held my breath, eyeing the ripples, then leaping
from level ground, was suddenly adrift,
all at sea, toeing the waters of uncharted skin.

The Stick

Blessed are the flexible,
for they shall not be bent out of shape.

1

It was a length of garden cane intended for growth,
a strip of bamboo, staked with ties to the soil.

Spring loaded with fixed intent, it could hoist
a flowering vine out of the tangles of knotted briar

and tame the midsummer creepers with its hard
unwavering line. Whip-like and limber,

unyielding as it had to be, it was an instrument
of my mother's affection, a measure of untold burden,

of tautened coil and twine, rooted in living memory
and dished out through the acts of labour and devotion.

It worked like a charm and I stared with frozen
watchfulness whenever she took it into her hand.

2

Then up and away we ran,
scattering in all directions,
bolting hell-for-leather
and running the gauntlet

through the halls of the house,
occasionally copping
razory slashes at the back
of the heels and knees,

before kicking back
and sticking our hands out,
while freeing the stiffened
key lock at the back of the door.

3

Once, when my mother was sleeping,
I took the stick into my own hands,
playing with its tension to see how far

it would bend. I laid it flat like a spirit level
and with all my boyhood strength
brought its top and tail ends down,

hoping that every shard of its tensile magic
would shatter from its glacial core.
I wanted to hear its threshold break,

to see each splintered half lying broken.
I wanted to turn it from a mother-child wand
into the image of an earthborn gift.

Heirloom

after Thomas Hardy's Heredity

Not a jewel or a thing you can touch,
the inherited keepsake stored deep in a box.
It is more the surmise of an inclination
that lingers under the surface like a clue.

At times it seems to cast itself without a trace
and leaves you second guessing the mirror.
You scan the lens of your eye, the lines on your face,
for a reflection of that inborn self,

that ancestral other—whose intangible source
you sense by impulse, like shoots of an under-level earth.
Sprung in roots it resurfaces, its absence disappears,

sometimes lurking beneath your breath,
or otherwise staring at you blindly, yet always
emerging within the clot of hidden transparencies.

Dolls

At fifty my mother started to collect dolls.
They weren't porcelain or Venetian.
They were cheap and most likely made in China.

She bought them from Flemington Markets
on a Sunday, where she happily binged amid
the chaos of want and waste, of trade and wonder.

At home they sat in prams, propped up in corners
of our old bedrooms. She started shortly after Cory died
and they multiplied when my brother and I left home.

I first noticed them on the days I went to see her,
the in-between days when she wasn't on dialysis.
I remember her lying on the bed, spent and exhausted.

The veins in her arms were so gnarled and swollen
from the treatment that whenever they were bare
I didn't know whether to speak or look away.

Once she rolled up her sleeves to show me.
I felt helpless and could only offer a silent nod.
Later we talked and I began tests for the transplant.

In the week she died, I visited twice. The first
was a Sunday. I remember how she stopped and smiled,
how she leaned on the step, arthritic in her middle years.

Tuesday was the last. I tidied up, unpacked the groceries
then sat beside her on the bed. She said, "When I die,
I've left money for you and your brothers beneath the dolls."

Swept

a valediction

Each with a wooden box and a broom,
my brother and I swept a car park
most nights of the week after school.

My mother had the good sense
to prepare us early for a life of work.
She got us the job, saved half our wages,

drove us back and forth each time.
'It's labour for liberty,' she'd say—
a life-like story of struggle

and dream, a poem of ode and elegy.
Stanley Plumly wrote—*in the parable,*
like the dream, you're all the characters,

though come the day, in real life,
you must choose. In every tell-tale
stitch of my inner fabric is a twinning

layer of loss buried beneath one truth;
I push and shove, the sound of sweeping,
when burying the lug, I carry the dream.

Switch

The telephone had been disconnected.
I called from another landline to reconnect.
I was put through the mill of transferring etcetera
and was asked to hold the line.
                                            I shut my eyes
for a moment in light relief, then leaned forward,
hunching over the table, determined to keep still.

A certain silence grew within me—
an inwardness that only seemed to inflate.
And almost at once, as if he had entered the room—
the low level sound of my father's breath.

2

Magpies

Easily mistaken as unearthly
yet far more grounded
than otherworldly,

poised and counterpoised
on two taut limbs,
strolling the parks,

perusing the suburban
networks of roads
and neighbouring reserves,

going about things
like a sentinel or an overseer,
composed and unperturbed

in befitting vestures
of black and white.
Each with three toes forward

and one toe back, walking
with wings tucked in at the hip,
stopping on lawns,

chattering in burble,
prodding and digging the earth
for embedded worms.

Or else breaking the high
summer air with lo-fi warbles,
wood-piped notes,

balancing rhyme and reason
from every high-topped
vantage point close to home.

Fierce keepers of the nest,
stoic guardians of their young.
Princely and proletarian,

they set with purifying
logic the clear-cut
divisible modes of grey.

The Fall

for Ella

I can tell you, when your horse began to slip
she tried to pull you and herself back up.
But once she slid and lost her footing,
you both fell into the realm of gravity
and came down hard upon the rain-soaked grass.

And in that moment, under the shockwaves
of a cold calm, I froze then ran with fear
as the freeze-frames reeled out—
you lying, pinned to the ground,
bearing the weight of your fallen mare.

At your side, I looked into the flared
whites of your eyes and calling your name,
watched your body tremble then jolt into a fit.
My heart sunk with a despairing dread,
a silent scream—*Not you, not now.*

I stayed kneeling, wondering whether
you were holding your breath or trying to breathe.
I scanned for bruising, broken bones, for blood.
I counted the seconds of your oblivion
and in a blind panic, even thought of prayer.

But when your body discharged a volt
with a kick and you spoke, surfacing to air,
I cupped my hands beneath your head,
spelling out the calm and colour of words.
As I held you on this side of the line that balances

love and loss with life and death, I pictured
your brother slipping by immeasurable degrees
through air and water, and thought of the ceaseless
eye of grief glaring at your mother and father.
By then, it didn't matter that the stir

and gaze of onlookers had crowded in
or that the spinning blades of a helicopter
throbbed overhead. What mattered was closer
to ground, and that the names of those you called
were there or on their way. Your horse,

limping, pressed her nose through a huddle
of bystanders, and with all the common
naturalness that comes from the animal bond
of love and need, tenderly bent to sniff
at your face, as you lay there in the wet

like a newborn foal. Walking back to the spot
later and seeing the muddy relief of your heel
near the hoof prints that lead toward your own,
I stood weighing up the cost, wondering
if it was luck or misfortune, or whether the law

of averages was simply taking stock of its toll.
I thought of how lucky you were and despite
the risks, remembered your overriding words,
"It's in my blood," and how every bone
within you has been marrowed by what it loves.

Villanelle for a Calf

I can still remember the sound.
The calf fell in, the gates shut hard.
I turned my eyes toward the ground.

He could hardly move or turn around
and was woken to truth there in the yard.
I can still remember the sound.

They said he was in the right way round
but he looked so stiff and awkward.
I turned my eyes toward the ground.

His body shook, his head flung round,
his mouth drooled wailing for his herd.
I can still remember the sound.

The farmhand didn't seemed to mind
the blood. The tools he said were standard.
I turned my eyes toward the ground.

He put on his glove and held the brand
out over the fire. I watched without a word.
I can still remember the sound.
I turned my eyes toward the ground.

Guinea Fowl

With a quail-shaped body
and a vulture-like head
they look like crossbred turkeys
or blue-ribbon hybrid hens.
Though in the kingdom of birds
this seemingly assorted
mixed bag is an independent flock
who, in slate-dark plumage
and moony-bright spots,
quills that a milliner would crave,
scratch around like Miss Marple,
stealthy as barnyard cats.
Nimble-footed in stifling
frocks, shrewd and antisocial,
they scour the land like ducks on water
but are nowhere near as quaint.
And they're far too busy
to swan about in a peacock suit
with the air of a lark ascending.
Theirs is the head down
hard-nosed blitz of unruly order,
driven as if by recompense or dutiful need.
In a gregarious grey-cloud tumbleweed
tight-knit pack, they've come to rid
the paddocks of seasonal peril:
locusts, spiders, ticks
and old, bald-faced misery.
Together they're in their element,
relentlessly rummaging,

constantly bending and pecking,
rooted to the spot at hand
in fastidious delight.
They do not care for the manacles
of a bygone world: kingdoms
of a fallen age, empires in the dust.
It's the sovereign dirt beneath their feet
and the babble of whistling chirps,
the workaday nod and lancing of beaks
that sets them apart from the hunt
in the grass.
                    As for the snake—
out from its pit of a hollowed log,
uncoiled as the rays of the sun,
needling through the underbrush
like a thick plait rivering in swards of green,
craving, I suppose, to slither head-on
into the banquet on the henhouse floor—
morning has lured it into the open,
freed it from the nocturnal swoop
of an owl and the hunt of a ravenous fox.
And as dawn unfurls in swathes
of random order, cold-blooded
with earthly hunger, the snake
slides-on, red tongue hissing,
a slick of fire across the feral sprawl.
Though in the eye of the guineas
it's merely a link in the chain of pests.
They'll spot one wriggling
in the burning distance or coldly
stalking under hot-flushed straw.
Then one by one they band together,
surround it in encircling ranks,

and with machinery screeches
they scourge in a cross-fire attack,
butchering it from head to tail
until the snake twitches
like a severed limb. And through
the punctured scales of its deathly skin,
in holes where there once were eyes,
they riddle it over with jackhammering pecks
leaving nothing more than a plaything,
bones for the driveling wind.

The Pigeons

In pink bow ties and green pashminas,
the pigeons stumble in a grizzled herd
and fly from where the council workmen
wash away the dried-up dung
which has piled like dirty snow
beneath the purple canopy
of St. John's...
                    Poor pigeons,
they were simply looking for a place to lay
their rotten eggs.

Snail

Hard and delicate, I am a garden snail.
　　My eyes are on the ends of tentacles.

I keep the peace and persist on insistence and will.
　　Such are my virtues. My aim is true.

I hold no grand illusions. I wear no purple robes.
　　Though let it be said that I am the spirit

animal of many endeavours. And although
　　I have left my prints all over your money tree,

I am by no means after your green. In my book,
　　distinctions of race and gender hold no currency.

I am a garden snail. The spiral of infinity
　　is my one and only, my golden mean.

In sunlit hours, I bear down for medallions of sleep.
　　The small hours of night are my domain.

I haul my humble camper up and down the highway.
　　My propensity to soldier on and never tire

I owe to the rain. For when I come out of my shell,
　　sluggishly as I do, it is with the fortuity

of hindsight that I shall pause within the teeming depths
　　and graze in the garden bed of my slow struggle.

The Echidna

1

Since the dawn of the Paleocene,
having lost its fins
and gained its spines,

Echidna surfaced from water to land,
clawing a way out of arid beds,

of bay and estuary,

and on mole-like feet,
waddled past the bones of dinosaurs.

2

Quickly,
        and on-all-fours,

it took to the earth
with the water-bound ease of a platypus

and in sharp defense,
                    passive survival,

bored a foot-deep evolutionary burrow
for long stints of life

in the slow lane.

3

Camouflaged in scrubby pixels
of pine cone brown,
                    this shambling thicket,
small bundle of tinder
wandered,
            a solitary nomad
seeking earth's concealment,

subsisting under rock, root and forest floor,

crepuscular,
            matutinal,
                        vespertine.

4

Over long seasons,

survival meant a coming to grips
with the twinning poles of hunger and refuge.

It insisted on buckling in
and burrowing under,

called for excavation on the spot.

It meant transformation,
the achievement of something specific...

Hatchling after hatchling,
the furless plump Buddha at birth

became the stout-limbed
bulldozing
        little doer
                of the ground,

the site-specific excavator
                of the underground.

5

With puggle born itty-bitty,
pink-skinned,
blind,
        preservation and hibernation
ruled
        as the two bright stars
of Mother Echidna's chart.

Inured to endure,
                she was on a mission,

scanning the breadth of her home range,
hunting with snuffling nerve,

poking
her nose into fallen logs,
                        turning wood
and leaf litter,

rummaging sunup to sundown,

foraging without play.

6

Weathering a bungalow of newfound spines
Echidna went on,
                    in slow evolution,

shuffling in a crown of thistles,

spur-born out of ebbing inland tides—

and barbed
            in its kingdom
                            of gold-tipped thorns.

Horse

Bending to the earth, the silhouette of a horse
is a hillside, dense as almond wood.
From wither to tail, a bristling escarpment
drops to a levelling range and a broadening flatland,
its bare-blank spine, cradles the sprawling horizon
and valley depths. At first light, with the long
slope of its neck plunging groundward,
it stands steaming among the outcrops,
thawing with the quartz-stone earth.
As the sun lifts, the mist comes quietly,
idly avalanching the treetops before draining
into the white void of the morning air.
On ironed hooves and crooked stumps, the horse
stays grazing, dipping and disappearing into itself.
Frostmelt drips from the red-brown furrows of its hide
down into the mud and clover.
                              Blowing in from the tops,
the air shifts and stirs; long flanks of light
strip shadows from the clay. Dozy, not asleep,
the horse sinks further into a wilderness within its skull.
How easily it drifts, stooped under such tonnage,
poised and unmoved in its thickly-furred, slack frame.
Motionless, under half-closed lids it has slipped,
as if flown from the bars of an unlocked gate,
bolted to the blind spot between its eyes,
dawning headlong deep in the dew.

3

Solar Lunar

after Douglas Dunn

The spinning drag of the sun and moon
work a tandem of orb and arc.

Day unspools into night and Earth revolves
to the synchronous hands of a clock.

In a dance between gravity and space,
the stars and planets have shifted overnight,

whirling in a do-si-do. Day-in, day-out,
we move as the world moves, through phase

and discourse, shade on shade, the bright rhythms
in sync with the dark degrees of under-goings.

The Juggler

Beneath the perpetual orbit
  of spinning worlds, haphazardly
    balanced upon the east-west

axis of a rocking plank,
  a man juggles a quintet
    of earth's most principal form.

Five glittering orbs go up,
  willing the onlookers awake
    as the spinning trajectory

arcs and cascades in a formula fit
  for theorems of geometry,
    or the mute notation of plotted

notes graphed in the minds
  of those who map them out
    across the horizontal lines of a stave.

A Ladder

Now can you see the monument?
—Elizabeth Bishop

Leaning against the wall,
    this wooden one
looks like an archetypal relic,

    sum-of-its-parts, offcut
or overhang salvaged from a rooftop,
    tree-house or a bridge.

Yet could there be anything
    more sound or as singular,
more fixed with sequential

    grace and pure symmetry?
Mantle of wood or template of air,
    trellis and framework of absolutes.

Foothold that permits you to step
    beyond the threshold of the here
and now—to haul the anchored

    freight of yourself to a vista
of probable clearances. Upwards
    you climb, rung upon level rung,

    strung between two landings,
though scaling madly into ascension
    as if the world were put on hold.

The Ring

for Cinnamon Lee
in memory of Robert Foster

When you find yourself in that moment,
and you're standing on the borderline

between what is given and what is gained—
think of the object at hand, the hard neutrality

and inner spark of the impartial diamond.
Think of it as hearthstone in relief,

an element whose steely light outweighs the sun,
whose opposing dark is the pure measure of tough love.

Bring to mind the very image of its hidden flame,
the way its obdurate force is concealed within,

how the wick of its enduring fires, locked-in
like an ember, is the one shining constant at the core.

Only when the rough grain is made of inexorable
grit, do bright colours blaze in the afterglow.

The Sweet Science

From fly weight to heavy weight,
pound for pound, it's all ring craft
and range, a duck and weave, stick and move,
mind-fest of fractions, millimetres
and miles, foot-worked, round after round,
in the spur of the moment flurry,
thrown from sweet-feet sugar-gloved hands,
artfully taken, slipped and countered
in the dancing margin of degrees,
where the art of to be or not to be hit
is a waltz of toughing it out upon the canvas,
and the four corners of the ring,
an empty page, history about to be written,
has the high hands toe-tuned Joe Marvellous
looking for the slipshod guard,
the hoodied kid with blind hunger
who spat blood and never knew why,
the punch drunk thug on the loose,
contender on the up, promotor on the take,
the fox-trotting shaman in love with his shadow,
poetic pugilist, testing his fitness for struggle
in the chin-grit, high stakes, take no prisoners,
ladies and gentlemen's game of punch and counter anticipation,
of being tagged and rocked but ever pressing forward,
where the odds-on bet of stomaching the air being knocked
out of you, swallowing the sting on your face,
taking it on the chin while channelling the movements of a panther,
a March hare, Roy Jones Jr. or Sugar Ray,
is a heightened sense of touch and intuition,

tactile sensitivity, a crafty concoction of shots on the inside,
the spatial awareness within a shrink-wrapped guard,
like the artful dodger slipping the big hitting old fella
who's in it for the dollar, not the distance,
nor the pain and process of drilling techniques
in numbing repetition, balancing the hardest blows
behind the lines, away from the hook, the haymaker,
the low blow, the clinch and the neutral corner,
away from the cutman and the crowd
toward the inner fusion of a knowing combo,
a minor major miracle of self vs. self, hardened fortitude,
the walk the talk coercion into coalescence, practiced precision
in the undisputed dance to undergo and overcome.

Stilled

after the still life paintings of Jude Rae

Substance takes form
in the guise of cups,
jugs, bowls and bottles,
taller half-hidden modes

that tremble blue, green.
At a distance, a glance,
the room feels hit upon,
unanticipated, as if by chance,

like standing in the doorway
of an attic, where on entry
you move with a stark
sense of quiet and isolation.

Perhaps it is nothing more
than a sudden awareness,
the mind's gift of lining its walls
with a blank yet brittle silence.

Here a jar, the containers,
even the grain of a table's edge
seem to reverberate in the mute
dust-fall of light and shade.

And there, not far, in a blur
of the out of reach: a slow
claim, the brushed brightness.
Sheer blaze of inaudible air.

Early Autumn

after Li Po

Early autumn, and the leaves gather at my feet,
a march of echoes is heard underfoot.
Digging deep, the earth reveals the heavens,
leaves spiral in a stellar wind then slowly drop.
I bow down among the labouring trees
and gather a sudden peace...
                              Had I known
that summer's green blood held the gold
of an autumn bloom, I'd have set green leaves
on fire and bowed down to you, deep autumn.

This Leaf

after Jo Shapcott

which whittled through rock,
which curved like a woodworm
within fissured stone, burrowing
within its division, its line of fault,

otherwise known as this stone's flaw.
Otherwise known as vein and pulse,
doubling up within tree-ring wood,
doubling up within fruitless stone.

This tunnelling through sap and grain
and seam. This resinous sinking
and rising through word and note.
This leaf, this wood, this stone.

A Crow

after Ted Hughes

As the wind ransacked every tree
and the storm hit,
the crow let out its *caw caw caw*.

It did not panic or stir
but drew on its cold skill,
a charring held darkly within.

And when it sprang from the branch,
flaring from claw to wing,
it flew up then shot off

into the sea-grey torrents of cloud,
knowing nothing of luck nor fear,
knowing nothing would be left to chance.

Ode and Elegy

after John Donne

Eden fell to grief and desire;
and there all the world is kept.

I awoke in the Garden of Eden,
for fear of loss I have not slept.

4

Road to La Masiera

It is good to be on the patched
and potholed road among the diesel cowboys,
toxic utes and earth-churned air.
Here, everything's rich with intention
or at ease with the lack of it: car-lot farmyards
loaded with Bedford trucks and block-bound F100s,
weed-fringed shipping containers and sunken
caravans, rusting with gypsy dreams.
Cluttered in jumble and strewn
with scrap for the tip, the whole place brims
with a collective shrug: loose-fenced paddocks,
trailers, boats and corrugated tin lie side by side.
And like a troupe of the nonchalant,
the locals fish out of dams under beach umbrellas
while a herd of cows stand up to their teats,
cooling in tea-coloured water.
Wherever you look, sprawling flat vistas
are dotted with ramshackle sheds, chicken farms
and quasi-palatial brickyard homes. Look,
here comes The Big Chook and here come those
Corinthian pillars, larger than the history of Greece.
Droll and bewildering, palm trees and cactus plants
add a certain continental colour to the roadside.
You could say it's all hotchpotch and mutton stew,
a Mediterranean Texas among the gums.
Goats and llamas, bedizened with flies,
are herded within a trove of worn-out tyres,
metal debris and Florentine statuettes.
The mix of warmth and neglect has their teeth

glinting yellow in the sun. In this Eden
of fountains and phoney flamingos, a lame horse
drinks from the troughs of replenished cloud.
On hillocks of backhoed dirt, somnolent birds
roost and flutter up, sifting the earth.
They peck at the roasted sprouts of wildflower
and sun-fed weed, dig into whatever else has taken
root through the drifts of heat and hothouse rain.

To a Horseman

for B.B.

I'm sitting on the fence watching you,
and I like how you go about things,
how you operate from a feel.
You seem to have turned on a light
in this troubled colt, going from pressure
to release, bringing him on, not breaking him.
You lead him away then ease him back in.
He drops his neck without a whinny,
and suddenly you say—*there's a change*—
but soon his flanks fire-up,
he whips his head and tail around,
trailing off with flaring nostrils,
and baring teeth. Though calmly
you persist, working in tandem,
with telling intuition. Your gestures say,
I am listening and I am not going to hurt you.
You offer a horse the regard to speak for itself.
Horses award you ribbons in their dreams.

At Willabah

Walking the long trodden path
toward the dam, I hear pebble
stones squelch underfoot and the wooden
jetty over the brown spangled water
pulse with the crooning of frogs.
At the foot of the landing, thick tangles
of grass, green on the blade,
flaxen like wheat at the tips, shoot up
between the gaps of the planks
and through the middle of a weather worn
tyre tube. Lily pads brim in bright,
mottled stages of bloom and ruin.
They look like a drifting patchwork
of miniature parasols, each stem softly landed.
But they have risen from murky depths,
launched pea-green sails and hoisted
ceaseless bulbs into the warm flushes of air.
Late afternoon sunlight crosses the dam
and an undershot cloud of tadpoles
darts through the gold shallows.
At the first mellow hint of dusk
a hidden swarm of cicadas begin to rattle,
amplifying a reverberant pitch
that fills the place with a thronging charge.
Up on a stilted rack above the edge
of swampish ground, a large red canoe
lies heavily with its curved ends down.
It is mosquito-peppered and sun bleached
from bow to stern, has lain here long enough

for a community of insects and organisms to thrive.
Turning it over, I see a black spider
scurry across the length of the gunwale
then take shelter beneath a dry mud-caked
taper of weed stuck there on its side.
I lower the canoe gently off its perch
and drag it by the ring rope to the water's edge
before going back for the oars that lie
in a melded slurry of bog and grass.
Out over the dam, jutting there steadily,
the canoe hangs in the balance on and off the jetty.
I lift it from its back end, tipping the scales.
It slides with a sudden splash, and in an instant,
wavelets swish into tremolo then recoil,
whitewashed in dissolving pools.
I ease myself into the vessel
and wait until the rocking ceases...
Tideless, the water is a reflecting threshold
of the bottomless blue, a blank scroll
glazed with a long shot sequence of idle air
and suspended inland sky. I set off,
levering the blade-end of the oar and row on
before letting the canoe drift and curve,
then run aground into the twig-ends of a white,
overhanging tree. As night sinks in, blue lit,
draining the heat, the searing horde of cicadas
gradually dims and smoulders with a resinous hum.
Still, there is enough light, enough shadowless
dark out here to stay and float, hammocked,
on this iridescent bed of backwater.
I let the oar slip, the canoe slide, and soaking
it all up, hold my hands out to the sudden rain.
Now, the dam, doused in nightfall,

magnetically blackens and seeps like a fumarole.
I lean back, immersed in a brightening shroud.
Cutting through the thick of it and crossing the haze,
I gape while lying dumbstruck under stars.

Tent

Pinned-down dwelling place,
small abode. Windsock
weathervane, umbrella home,
where I lie lodged
as the night, lunar-bright,
comes quickening.
I wake and look out
through an eyelet no bigger
than a loophole.
Earth has turned its cheek
to the moon's and the distance
blinks with a clot of stars.
I reach up and feel
for the switch
on the hanging lamp.
The air brightens with a click
then dims to a tarnished glow.
Out in the paddock
all four corners
of the ground have vanished
and the earth-melded sky
glints in a freeze-frame
of mica and aeon-blasted light.
I walk on toward the river
under the constellations
of spun glitter.
The blackened trees
and edgeless hills are all
but gone from view. I listen

to the long bowed heads
of horses ripping fattened tufts
from the earth. Their shoes
are loose and clackety
and they move with an easy gait.
Now the moon is above the river,
iridescent in its powdery shell,
sinking low on the horizon
and tiding in ripples downstream.
I keep watch, locked
to the tumbling current,
and imagine the hidden fish
coursing in snowmelt and silt.
Beneath them, the river
drags its stones over and over,
dredged and shovelled
along for an age,
submersed in a stony elixir.
Beyond the slow rising pools
the river meanders, spilling
its pebbles and shale.
On the banks a cold thin crust
forms over the grass. I hear
a crumbling beneath my boot soles.
I walk back to the tent
as the domed world sleeps.
The rain falls. I lie listening
to the petering bell of a cricket
and cling to its residual note.

Acknowledgements

Acknowledgements are due to the editors of the following journals and anthologies in which some of these poems have previously appeared: *Antipodes, Cordite, Island, Meanjin, Snorkel, The Weekend Australian Review, The Canberra Times, The Red Room online, Westwords, Collective Tissue, Newcastle Poetry Prize 2015 Anthology, All These Presences, 2016 Anthology, On First Looking, 2018 Anthology, Best of Australian Poems Anthology, 2014 & 2017.*

'Stilled' was first published in *Drawn to Form: The Matter in Hand, exhibition catalogue, Blacktown Arts Centre, 2015.*

'The Stick' was first published in Substitute: *The Untold Narrative of a Mother & Son, exhibition catalogue, Abdullah M.I. Syed. Fairfield City Museum and Gallery, Sydney, 2016.*

Special thanks to Judith Beveridge, Stephen Edgar, Emma Fielden, Robert Gray and David Musgrave.

'Shade on shade' in the poem 'Solar Lunar' is from Douglas Dunn's poem 'Summer Night'.

www.ingramcontent.com/pod-product-compliance
Lightning Source LLC
Chambersburg PA
CBHW031005090426
42737CB00008B/690